Firefighter

Quarto is the authority on a wide range of topics.

Quarto educates, entertains and enriches the lives of our readers—enthusiasts and lovers of hands-on living.

www.quartoknows.com

First published in hardback in the UK in 2009
by QED Publishing
Part of The Quarto Group
The Old Brewery,
6 Blundell Street,
London, N7 9BH

A catalogue record for this book is available
from the British Library.

ISBN 978 1 84835 252 0

Printed and bound in China

Author Amanda Askew
Designer and Illustrator Andrew Crowson
Consultants Shirley Bickler and Tracey Dils

Publisher Steve Evans
Creative Director Zeta Davies
Managing Editor Amanda Askew

Words in bold are
explained in the
glossary on page 24.

Firefighter

Amanda Askew
Andrew Crowson

QED

Meet Jack. He is a firefighter.
He helps to make places safe
from fires. He also puts out fires.

Jack arrives at the fire station
and he changes into his uniform.

At the fire station, Jack wears a blue uniform. When there is a fire alarm, Jack puts on a fire suit, a helmet and heavy black boots.

His uniform lets people know that he is a firefighter.

5

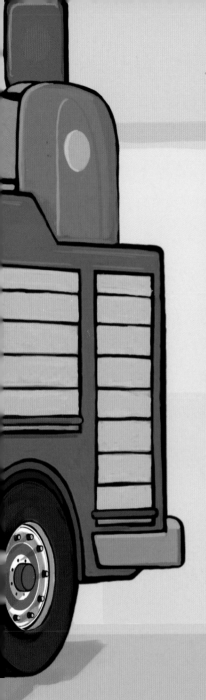

Joe, the **Watch Manager**, checks that all six firefighters are there.

First, Jack and the other firefighters have to make sure that everything is working properly when the **alarm** bells go off.

"Everyone's here. Let's start checking and cleaning the truck," Joe says.

Later that morning, Jack fits a new **smoke alarm** for Mrs Patel. He shows her how to use it properly.

"You need to check that it works once a month by pressing this red button. You must also change the batteries twice a year."

"Ok, thanks," Mrs Patel says.

9

Jack goes back to the station for lunch.
Just as he's finished his sandwich...
RING, RING, RING!
It's the fire alarm.

Jack and the other firefighters put on their helmets and rush to the fire truck.

"Dover Street School.
There's a fire in
the kitchen,"
Joe shouts.

Jack drives and puts on the siren so other cars on the road will move out of the way.

When they arrive at the school, the children are standing quietly in the playground. There is smoke coming from the building.

Carl talks to the teacher
to find out what happened.

"Is anyone trapped in the building?"
Carl asks.
"No, all 75 children are out."

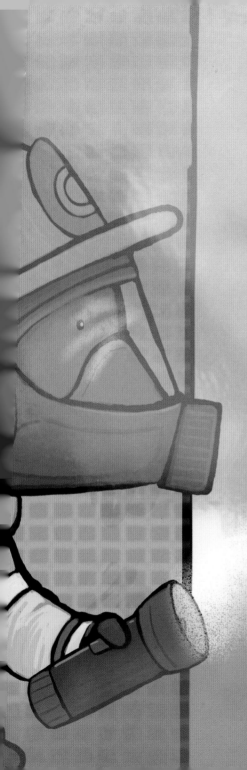

Jack, Peter and Lucas put on **air masks** so they can breathe properly. They crash through the kitchen doors.

They can hardly see because the smoke is black and thick.

"Look! It's coming from the ovens." They spray water onto the flames until, at last, the fire is out.

Outside, Jack and Lucas put the hose away.

Peter and Max look to
see what started the fire.
They also check that
the building is safe
before everyone can
go back inside.

"Thank you for coming so quickly," the teacher says. "Not a problem!"

Jack feels a tap on his arm. "Please, sir, can we climb on your fire truck?"

22

Jack laughs. "Not today. Maybe another time!"

Glossary

Air mask Something that covers your face and gives you extra air to breathe.

Alarm Equipment that makes a loud warning noise.

Siren Equipment that makes a loud warning noise. It is usually used on fire trucks, police cars and ambulances.

Smoke alarm Equipment that makes a loud noise when there is smoke or fire in a building.

Station Place where fire officers work.

Uniform Type of clothing worn by fire officers.

Watch Manager The officer in charge of the fire station and the other fire officers.